THOT

CHANTÉ L. REID

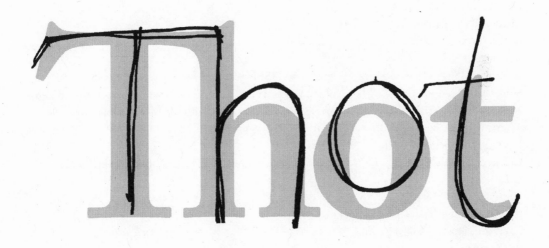

Thot

Sarabande Books
Louisville, Kentucky

Publisher's Cataloging-In-Publication Data
(Prepared by The Donohue Group, Inc.)

Names: Reid, Chanté L., author.
Title: Thot / Chanté L. Reid.
Description: [Louisville, Kentucky] : Sarabande Books, [2022] | Includes bibliographical
references.
Identifiers: ISBN 9781956046113 (paperback) | ISBN 9781946448224 (ebook)
Subjects: LCSH: Reid, Chanté L.--Childhood and youth. | Reid, Chanté L.--Education. | Women
authors--United States--Biography. | Women graduate students--Rhode Island--Biography. |
Morrison, Toni. Beloved. | Bronx (New York, N.Y.)--Social conditions. | LCGFT: Autobiographies.
| Creative nonfiction.
Classification: LCC PS3618.E532 Z46 2022 (print) | LCC PS3618.E532 (ebook) | DDC 813/.6--
dc23

Cover design by Sarah Flood-Baumann.
Interior design by Danika Isdahl.
Printed in Canada.
This book is printed on acid-free paper.
Sarabande Books is a nonprofit literary organization.

This project is supported in part by an award from the National Endowment for the Arts. The
Kentucky Arts Council, the state arts agency, supports Sarabande Books with state tax dollars and
federal funding from the National Endowment for the Arts.

THOT

I.

I heard a gunshot so close I checked my body for its wounds. It wasn't a panicked search. I was staring at a computer, writing a paper on Beloved. I was quite in love with both Denvers and no bullet wound was going to distract from that so I touched myself as though I were searching for a wallet. I went: right thigh pocket left thigh pocket hoodie-pouch over stomach pocket, left cheek pocket, right cheek pocket, all while staring at a screen reworking a sentence, an argument:

Toni Morrison's Beloved demonstrates
               catalyzes
               portrays Denver as an image of queer futurity through
                                       by
                                     ;meaning, the circumstances
                                           retelling—

And then I heard another gun shot so I left the sentence incomplete and walked over to my mother's front door, looked through the peephole and re-performed the wallet-search, before returning to the paper with a lost train, and needing to go elsewhere:

E.B House and other critics
House and Joyner
Common readings of Beloved argue
               question whether or not
               analyzes
               posits Beloved, the character
                       the woman
                             the corporeal figure as ghost and unpacks
                                      explores

analyzes what properties

characteristics

powers

truths of 'ghosts'

'ghosthood'

speak to Beloved's performance on both the story and thematic level; however, I'd like to offer

Beloved, to me,

reads as vampire—

Here, my mother comes home from work, disturbs the sentence and a conversation ensues:

The police killed somebody.

What do you mean, here, now?

They say it was the lady downstairs

A lady in the lobby?

No. The lady that lives downstairs.

Mad ladies live downstairs, Ma. When and where.

Girl, are you listening? Here. Thee Lady that lives downstairs.

Danner?

Girl, you know I don't know anyone's name, but yeah I think so. The one that's usually on her terrace yelling, Crazy—

Don't call her crazy, Ma.

How'd I know you were going to tell me I couldn't her call by what we've been calling her. All of a sudden you know her name.

Not all of a sudden.

All of a sudden. It's a damn shame and it shouldn't have happened but don't get holier than thou on me. All the time: 'Ma I can't read 'cause Crazy is yelling, Ma, I can't hear the TV, Crazy is screaming, Ma, guess what Crazy said to me in the elevator' and now, all of a sudden you know her name.

I been knew her name, I just know you don't know anybody's name.

Surprised you were home this whole time and didn't hear anything.

I heard
flinched
checked myself
was writing a story
            paper.

You were writing a paper. Can't hear when your eyes are busy, huh?

Can't see if my ears are listening.

Snarky—don't cut off your nose to spite your face little girl. What's the paper about?

I don't know

Beloved
Medea
Vampires
Image
Futurity
Time and space
I don't know—stuff
Books and shit.

Books and shit? Okay, well it's your pockets this time.

It's my pockets this time.

II.

Paper
Story
Writing, interrupted
       distracted by my mother
             the police
             my body
             Danner
             The Bronx
             the police
             my mother, but still
                     despite, Beloved
                       Medea
                       my mother
                       the police
                       the Bronx
                       my pockets
                       this time, remains on my mind. Interrupted fragments
and reworked sentences like shards of glass, piercing
                    stabbing
                    staking. A ruptured cup
                            vase
                            mirror
                            light bulb
                            window
                            pane of parts never quite

connected. Visible glue and staples, missing the proper transitions and citations like 'however'

'also'

'furthermore'

'(Morrison

124)'

'Lacan asserts'

'(Marks 67)'

'contrarily,'

forgetting to pray to new and old gods

creators

authors. Instead I offer memories

briefs

fragments

shards in exchange for peace

sound

contiguity

continuance

fortitude

rest.

III.

Thot is a slang-word
                epithet
                (n)acronym primarily used against a woman
                                         girl
                                         lady
                                                -identifying person
                                        person who looks to other people as though
they could be aligned with femininity

                                      vampire. It stands for two things simultaneously,
conflated for speech
                time
                bevity—The Hood Owns That, That Hoe Over There.

I no longer attempt to offer arguments
                            conclusions
                            reasoning
                            explanations so I leave because the police
                                                        my mother
                                                         vampires
                                                        ghosts
                                                        Medea
                                                        Beloved has shown me, I'm not an

argument

conclusion-type; however, I still check my body

        mother

        neighborhood for bullet wounds

                images

                shadows

                associations

                shards

                stakes, hoping to find love

empathy

understanding, hoping to never make any conclusions

        judgments about ghosts

           women

           my mother

           vampires

           Thots. Except the police. *Fuck*

The Police, a rap song by acclaimed rappers N.W.A and in high school

        at St. Vincent's, I'm sent home on

dress-down day for wearing this acronym on a t-shirt. The Dean of Discipline

        Police

        Authority

        Vice Principal, a former Bronx resident

                Thot

                neighbor

                stranger

misuses inside knowledge to determine I'm breaking a profanity

        curse

        language rule.

The conversation:

That's inappropriate.

N, W, and A?

You and I both know what that means.

You mean, like, it means something or it stands for something?

Go home, Chanté.

Can't you just call my parents, or like—

No

What if I get my dad to bring me a different shirt?

No

C'mon, B.

What did you just call me?

That's a stretch and you know it. I didn't call you anything.

So how about you just go home, and this way you don't have to explain 'B' or any other letter to the sisters.

Only she would know

    think.

    believe that to be sent from school

        St. Vincent's

        65th & Lex to home

            The Bronx

            Castle Hill

            the hood would be punishment. Home

as punishment is

    was

    thought to be a tool

        sentence

        punishment

        weapon formed against me. In Fishkill, New York my father's mother

                                    an authority figure

resided and ran a house

      detention center

      reform school specifically for her offspring

              my wayward cousins

              me.

Throughout

Across   time

      loops, I'm sent to the pond

          Fishkill

          my grandmother's house for reforming

                  rearing

                  reformation.

IV.

Clips of conversations across

in that time

space:

Clip) *Do you know why I live so close to the prisons?*

No.

Good answer.

Clip) *There's no obedience in that—Do. Confess. Forgive. Do Confess Forgive. You won't ever be allowed to do, confess, and then expect to be forgiven so you might as well cut that out now.*

Yes.

Leaves and sticks and statues and candles—blasphemy.

Yes.

What type of church lets women go in slacks?

Yes.

Yes, you agree?

Yes, I hear you.

Fair.

Clip) *While we're in here, you get fifteen syllables. There's nothing you need to say to me that should take more than fifteen syllables.*

Can I ask a question before we go in then?

No you may not, and you've used twelve of your syllables.

Clip) *I told you three times to stop digging up my grass.*

Last summer, you said the grass was okay to play with
because it's dying and you're going—
That memory of yours is going to be the death of you. This is what I'm saying this summer. Stop pulling up my grass.

Fair, Old Lady.

Fair Old Lady? That's funny, Be funny with them others, not me.

Clip) *This is how you live to be my age.*

With all due respect, what if I don't want to live to be
your age?

Pulling up grass and telling jokes. You're hard-headed but, I think I love you.

I think I love you too, Old Lady.

V.

Another sentence:

To call Margaret Garner "The Modern Medea," suggests

                          re-contextualizes her namesake

                               predecessor

                               ancestor

                               progenitor. To liken Garner

                                          Sethe to Medea

is to admit

Euripides' *Medea* also tells the story of—

A voice

  editor

  cop

  peer

  Schoolteacher masquerading as friend

                     family

                     authority pulls me over for speeding

                               writing

                               running on the wrong side of the

road

paper. I hate

    dislike

    don't understand his name because it has too many meanings

                          definitions

                          synonyms

versions
references so I avoid the spiral
chaos
disorder
frenzy com-

ing by using silence
shards
syllables (no more than fifteen).

He says:

What is this?

What do you mean?

Who is your audience?

What do you mean?

Well, Tayari Jones has this quote that I think about with my own writing, and I'd like you to consider it—"I would never write a story my sister couldn't read" and I feel like your work loves white Gods and is therefore geared towards a white audience, not your sister, not me.

Word?

'Word?'

That means 'Really?' 'Are you sure?' in this particular context.

Oh. well then yes, 'Word.'

                    Where you from?

My grandparents were born in—

                    Nah man, like what neighborhood?

Between Ozone and Howard Beach.

                    Word.

Are you asking if I'm sure I'm from Queens?

                    Different cadence—not asking anything.

Point heard
    understood
        evaluated. I want to tell him about the relationship between coincidence

                    chance
                    providence
                    simultaneity
                    conjunction
                    fortuity
                    fate and assignment
                        designation
                        allotment
                        task
                        homework, but every-

thing I think to say sounds like exposition

explanation

excuse so I take this piece of criticism

condemnation

judgement like the champ

pussy

coward I am,

and I keep it moving.

VI.

A sentence:

It is not internal
    mental
       psychological 'madness' that propels the infanticide
                        suicide
                        action. Medea
                            Sethe exists
                            lives
                            mothers in 'mad' contexts
                                    settings
                                    squares and triangles
                                      and circles
                                shapes and, shift
                                      shape-shift
                                    to

For example, Sethe must sell
              re-sell her body for a tombstone
                      word, shifting to prostitute
                            scribe
                            Thoth
                            Thot
                            The Hood Owns That, That Hoe
Over There.

                          The neighborhood claims that, that

tool to be used in the shed.

        in the dark.

                        The context defines and determines
this object's specific subjectivity.

                        The place in which you live is re-
sponsible for you; you, who is irresponsible and slightly adjacent and therefore ostracized and
authorized.

                        The people that constitute the place
claim ownership of and are also responsible for the ostracized other whose body and presence
they benefit from but are ashamed of, and therefore, they keep it close, but keep it outside over
there in the dark

    in the shed

    under the moon.

A welcomed interruption from my mans

                friend

       Léo:

    Té, where you been?

                    Around man, around.

    Word? I ain't see you on the block in a minute.

I been on the block, but I haven't been on the block
at the same time.

I feel you, shit's wild out here. I'm trying to get like you, B.

You don't want to get like me.

Did you hear about Mike?

I saw it on *Bronx 12*. That was your mans. I'm sorry
but with his folks—how?

*Nah nah nah, that was your mans but that's exactly what I said—I was like if I had his parents,
I'd be like a lawyer or some shit. Homie graduated at the top of our class.*

"I went to Cheesecake, he was a *motherfucking waiter there.*
Alpha, step, *Omega*, step"—

Nah but for real, how's moms for you?

She's good. 60 hours a week still. How's your
grandmother?

*Getting on my fucking nerves. I told my pops I can't do this shit no more, somebody else gotta
take a shift. I don't care who—him, the pope, one of those uhm, like nurses that come to your
house—I don't care anymore. Yo' every day, B. 'Léo donde 'stá' 'Léo, I'm lonely' 'Léo this' 'Léo
that—' I'm a grown ass man, B. Anyway, how's your pops, he gave you the Expedition yet?*

My pops is dead. I didn't get the Expedition. My
moms lets me push her Rav 4 though.

You lying, B.

Everybody's always talking shit, but it's a good car—
good on gas, good in the snow, and my brother said

Yo' I'm talking about your pops being dead.

Oh. nah, I'm deadass.

You not deadass.

On my moms, I'm deadass, B.

'Moms'
'Pops'
'Mans'—singular but plural because when you know
love someone, you acknowledge
allow their multiplicity. Still,
even that note is another's voice creeping
explaining
bleeding onto the moment
memory
hood, explaining
exposing. In actuality, it's just how we talk
who we

are in private. When we hangup the phone, he texts me—*143*

an anachronism, from the days of beepers

before our time

for people without language

        time

        space

        the capacity to say 'I love you,' making me wonder

question

ask whether it truly is an anachro-

nism if we are still people without language

        time

        space

        the capacity to say 'I love you.' I text back—143, B

I love you too,

friend

Léo de la ghetto , a nickname given to Léo

        , a nickname given to Léo before

when we're young

outside

inside

playing in parks

on courts

in hoods

homes like ours where your name must announce what your body cannot. Like White Mikes which assumes there are other Mikes

                  Mikes who are not white

                        will have to answer for

                                explain

                                expose

                                excuse pink-lipped

                                      blue eyed boys who share our lan-

guage

space

time

capacity for love; however, I suppose, inherent in such a nickname and without knowing we were

doing so, we prepared

                anticipated

                expected future claims

                            accusations of appropriation

                                    passivity

                              failing to condemn

                                      acknowledge difference.

But again, appropriation is a now-word and Léo de la ghetto

                                is from before, and our

                                          this language will never be

stationary

set

still enough to give a true noun

                        word used to identify any of a class of people, places, or things—to condemn. It's all verb

    action

        movement, so dependent on context

            space

              time, requiring conjugation, used over there

                      this way

                      at this time

                      in the dark and

only ever with love.

In this way, through text

        on the phone, Léo de la Ghetto now too is just a ghost

                character

                voice—disembodied.

VII.

With time
    sex, Sethe purchases ceremony
        monument
        language.

Howard Beach tells
    sells me the noun
        term Black English
        African American Vernacular English
        AAVE, an acronym that's hard for my mouth because it sounds

like an anachronism
    hymn that misplaces my mind—
        Ave, and suddenly Léo de la Ghetto and I are
young
at Holy Family School
in a pew, playing
    performing
    pretending our closed fists in each other's faces hold microphones
        dicks and on each Ah, we swat
        push
        hit the

other's closed fist away from our own faces. Neither his closed hand in front of my face nor my closed hand in front of his are wanted, but the swat

        swing

        hit

        push with our free

            open

        other hand—that's what's fun

                amusing

                pleasurable.

              The authority

               dean of discipline

can't send us home

      to the hood like the authorities of the future will because we're already there

               here

               on Castle Hill

               Avenue

               home so

instead we receive warnings

        omens

        notices

    papers that read 'playing' to be signed

            authenticated

            endorsed by a parent

               guardian

               mother

               father

               grandmother to show they know

                   are

aware of what we've done

      been doing

      will probably do again and, what's coming

               the consequences

               repercussions

               tremors.

VIII.

The play's
      novel's historical
            mythical
            narrative tremors
                  echoes haunt which supports all readings that believe in ghosts
                                          apparitions
                                          punishment
                                          sin; how-
ever, there is the blood
                  feeding
                  focus on the neck
                        body.

A fractured
   forgotten memory between Léo and I:

      I got into the academy

                        The police academy?

   There's another type of academy?

                        Well, yeah man, there's dance academies, sports
                        academies, research academies—

—Bruh, what other type of academy am I built for?

                        You talking about predetermination?

Nigger, what?

                        You said you were built for this. You think you were always going to be a cop—no matter, what?

I'm talking about my build and my brain. Like, what else can I do?

                        I think we're talking about the same thing.

I think you bugging, B.

IX.

Bugging

Madness

Instability

Disorder

Mania—a natural symptom of being both owned and otherized, possessed. Taken out of context or trapped within—circus.

News reporters surround the building for weeks, asking about Danner

$\qquad\qquad\qquad\qquad\qquad\qquad$ rent

$\qquad\qquad\qquad\qquad\qquad\qquad$ noise complaints

$\qquad\qquad\qquad\qquad\qquad\qquad$ history.

Morrison used a clipping

$\qquad\qquad$ reference

$\qquad\qquad$ sliver

$\qquad\qquad$ rib

$\qquad\qquad$ bite of newspaper

$\qquad\qquad\qquad$ life to create Sethe and now Garner lives

$\qquad\qquad\qquad\qquad\qquad\qquad$ provides information

$\qquad\qquad\qquad\qquad\qquad\qquad\qquad$ fragments never known to

neighbors

strangers

me.

Deborah Danner was a poet

    essayist

    expert on madness

      racism and schizophrenia.

I just know some people:

        Yo'

How are you?

        So what are they saying?

Well, you gotta understand, B—

        Don't give me that shit, Leo

I'm still in blue and like they don't really talk around me like that cuz' I've already fucked up like mad times, my nigger like mad times. Like the other day, I was out with the sarge, and like he wanted me to give those kids that be up on L dancing a ticket right but I was like—
        Léon.

Damn, you hit me with the Léon like you my pops or my fucking boss or something. No love at all?

        I'm sorry.

That lady was bat-shit , B. She been bat-shit since we were little and you know that so like she swung on him. Suicide-by-cop.

Suicide-by-cop in her own fucking house? You
believing or reporting?

I mean—like, I'm just telling you what the station is saying, B.

What you saying tho?

I'm not saying shit. I'm just saying what's being said. What you trying to say, my nigger?

Don't call me a nigger, Leo

Why are you talking to me like I'm white—shit's just tragic.

That's crazy. I don't even talk to white people, at least
not on Sundays. Isn't today Sunday?

X.

As a tragedy, Euripides' *Medea* is strange. The titular character ascends

of Morrison's *Beloved*

comes up from the river one day.

I hear
  see
  feel buzz
      vibrations
      echoes
      Notifications
      headlines—*Tragedy in The Bronx* and a voice creeps

bleeds

reminds

calls on tragedies' requirements:

The first thing you learn in the studies of White Gods

Classics

Authorities, is that tragedies are for men. A Woman

Iphigenia

Alcestis

Beloved (the

baby) is a sacrifice
      offering
      surrender
      suicide

by cop
    authority
    King
    Schoolteacher.

As for hamartia
    flaw
    failure, I suppose Medea's mouth
            speech
            wit
            sex
            language incites conflict
                  climax
                  calls to the police
                  chorus
                  community. She is loud
                        boisterous
                        free and we
                            the

community
chorus
neighbors are jealous
        polite
        policed.

XI.

Morrison chooses to omit

        remove

        do-away with Sethe's boy

              other children immediately and offers little to

no explanation about their whereabouts

        futures. Like Halle

          their father—

Protestors chant

      join newscasters outside

        gathering

        demanding Justice for Deborah Danner. I join

                  whisper

                  type

                  chant to their rhythm and

accidentally summon Justice

        my brother:

You never pick up my calls.

             My fault. Happy Belated Birthday

Happy Belated Birthday to you too. Where have you been?

             Just Brooklyn and back. Start of the semester, and
             then I'm sure you heard.

Heard about what?

Really? it's all over the news—Deborah Danner.

Who's that?

Justice.

—Just tell me

Our neighbor, downstairs. The police busted in her crib last week and well, you know.

I don't remember her. How is it up there?

I suppose it's fine, same stuff you see whenever this happens.

Are you mad at me because I don't remember her? Last time I lived there, your front teeth hadn't even grown in yet.

I'm not mad.

You sound mad.

Justice.

Sethe's boys

        Howard and Buglar only exist in the past but Morrison never writes

                                                                   suggests death as

the reason

        cause for this particular absence. All we

                                the reader

                                chorus

                                community know is they are in some way free

                                                                     wander-

ing from 124

        Sweet Home

        this ghost.

Off the phone

Staring at the screen, I listen

                        hear the chants for Danner but I don't join

                                                    chant, now afraid of myself ability to

call

summon Justice

        my father who owes me an expedition.

XII.

Denver drinks the baby's blood, Sethe's milk and stays

> befriends
>
> braves
>
> protects the ghost
>
> house
>
> Sethe as though the blood
>
> milk

grants her immunity

> freedom

defenses against a draining

> feeding

vengeful past. Skipping a few generations

> centuries
>
> universes
>
> gods, she inherits Medea's mouth
>
> wit
>
> speech

and this time—

I pick up a phone call:

Can you talk to Amanda for me? She's tripping about twenty dollars and a t-shirt.

Why do you keep fucking up?

I mean if you think about it—it's not stealing if it's from your sister.

Word?

Straight Facts, B.

Facts is the new word?

Word is Facts for old people.

Facts, then.

This is Travis
    a brother
    an echo. He danced
        drew atop the 6
           on castle hill, received tickets
                warnings
                expulsions
                early dismissals too—uniform infractions.

I love
  talk to his sister.
      Amanda.

An echo:

You got sent home again?

Uniform infraction.

Chanté—it's dress-down day.

I know. If we still know each other when we're
grown-ups , I'll let you know when and how I get
fired on my day off.

You think you're going to have a job?

Hopefully not, B. Hopefully not. What about you, I
know you didn't get in trouble.

My brother—he likes to jump off of shit. Did it at school, hurt himself.

He likes to jump off of shit?

Girl, he just likes to jump off of shit. I don't know how to explain it.

Is he hurt bad?

You care?

I'm interested.

I guess I'll know when I get there—you want to come?

Hospital or school?

A school right by my house. St. Raymond's

On Castle Hill?

Yeah, you know it?

I'm from Castle Hill.

No you're not.

- Amanda, *no you're not.* You get off the 6 at 116th every day.

Babysitting job.

Bet, say less.

What's the NWA on your shirt about?

NWA. The rap group. You know? You gotta know. How you don't know, B—Fuck the police comin' straight from the underground / A young nigga got it bad 'cause I'm brown / And not the other color so police think / They have the authority to kill a minority—It's like from the '80s and shit.

So before we were born?

My pops likes music, hates the police.

Ah. The Sisters knew what that was?

Nah, Clickity-Clack Keys is from the Bronx.

She's not from the Bronx.

Girl, she's from Soundview.

XIII.

Paul D, in stereotypical
      archetypal Step-Dad
            parent fashion drives
                 expels
                 evicts the righteously unruly
                        angry
                        naughty
                        suffering
                        disobedient ghost
                              baby, and in her place
                                 from

the river rises Beloved. It wasn't his place
                  child
                  past or future to oust.

Travis jumps
      slips
      falls by accident
            while drawing
                dancing
      on purpose from the top of a building
                        construction
                        composition
                        establishment. All of twenty-two
                              years reduced to a jump
                                 slip
                                 fall. Characterized

and reduced by actions
        jumps
        moves. The why
           how—unnecessary
               unknown. He was always so clumsy, tiny Taurus
                         Bull in a china

shop, breaking things
        rules
        uniform infractions, getting expelled
               evicted
               thrown-out of institutions
                    by authorities
             placed into   institutions
                    by authorities.

Expulsion
Eviction
Expatriation exhaust
        make Sethe
           Medea
           Garner
           Danner
        ghosts mad too.

For Christmas, to prevent stealing
           borrowing
           sibling-entitlement, Amanda and I buy him clothes
                     shirts
                     pants

a coat, size small. Twenty-
two

22 and still a small;

a pair of shoes, size 11

that he never gets to wear because he falls

jumps

slips in January

the cold, barefoot

assed

naked.

A conversation between Amanda and I on shoes:

Should we sell them?

What does your mother want?

She wants us to deal with it.

What do you want?

He never wore them.

There's like this fake or like overused example of a
short-short story that's wild dramatic—

Baby shoes for sale—never worn.

How'd you know that?

Chanté.

What?

Just because I don't do what you do, doesn't mean I don't listen to you. You think this is the first time you've mentioned this thing?

Mad people think—

Yes, Yes, Hemingway but not. Pack the box, boo.

I'm sorry.

What were you going to say?

Well—dark joke. One Travis would appreciate.

Go ahead

Iight so I'll sell them right but like make the caption, baby shoes for sale, size 11—never worn.

I don't know if that's funny, but it is cute—thank you.

How much do you want to sell them for?

Something actually funny.

You mean like an exorbitant amount?

'You mean like an exorbitant amount'—just say large.

I'm being insensitive?

No, no. I'm just—

Well, of course.

How about 500, they're still unworn.

We should add a zero for sentimental value.

We should double that because they're unworn and sentimental.

Quadruple because I think I should be compensated for the funny of the joke.

Halve it then 'cause the joke is inaccessible.

The joke is mad accessible, B.

Alright, I take that back—inaccessible is unfair. Halve it because it's an inside joke.

I'd argue that that's a reason to double it.

'I'd argue that that's a reason to double it'—, Bitch, halve it for that.

Bruh. You got one more time before I hitback. You got away with two.

Okay, okay, add a zero for noticing.

What we at now?

500; 5000; 10,000; 40,000; 20,000; 200,000.

I'm putting it up now. Baby shoes for sale, size 11, never worn—$200,000.

Questions and comments from strangers about the ridiculous price:

Are these Kanye's personal pair?

Is this an unreleased color-way ?

You're a fucking scammer, nigger.

Resellers ruin the culture, B.

It's for my kid. Can you come down a little?

Bloodsucking ass bitch.

XIV.

Erasure's remedy is not inclusion—it is adornment, however illegible, however close to the edge. Graffiti, for example, is inherently gracious, indebted to structure, possible through support. In the great words of Naughty by Nature, *You down with O.P.P.? Yeah, you know me.*

*A vampire has to be invited in, let the
romance novels tell it.

like love. [1800 – 1850] for white men
like romantic period → the belief that migration all
europe ↳ subjectivity, individualism, spontaneity,
      ↳ freedom from rules, solitary life rather
         than life in society

Both five simultaneously occurring

Different [1800 – 1850]   Vampire → supernatural strength
America ↓

friend
invisible
ghostly

The Civil
War

BELOVED is my sister. I swallowed her blood right along
with my mother's milk. The first thing I heard after not hear-
ing anything was the sound of her crawling up the stairs. She
was my secret company until Paul D came. He threw her out.
Ever since I was little she was my company and she helped me
wait for my daddy. Me and her waited for him. I love my
mother but I know she killed one of her own daughters, and
tender as she is with me, I'm scared of her because of it. She
missed killing my brothers and they knew it. They told me
die-witch! stories to show me the way to do it, if ever I needed
to. Maybe it was getting that close to dying made them want
to fight the War. That's what they told me they were going to
do. I guess they rather be around killing men than killing
women, and there sure is something in her that makes it all
right to kill her own. All the time, I'm afraid the thing that
happened that made it all right for my mother to kill my sister
could happen again. I don't know what it is, I don't know
who it is, but maybe there is something else terrible enough to
make her do it again. I need to know what that thing might
be, but I don't want to. Whatever it is, it comes from outside
this house, outside the yard, and it can come right on in the
yard if it wants to. So I never leave this house and I watch
over the yard, so it can't happen again and my mother won't
have to kill me too. Not since Miss Lady Jones' house have I

slavery?
mystery
madness?

and it can come right on in if it wants to

She said no. She had hoped about an afternoon job at the shirt factory. She hoped than with her night work at the Bodwins' and another one, she could put away something and help her mother out. When he asked her if they treated her all right over there, she said more than all right. Miss Bodwin taught her stuff. He asked her what stuff and she laughed and said book stuff. "She says I might go to Oberlin. She's experimenting on me." And he didn't say, "Watch out. Watch out. Nothing in the world more dangerous than a white schoolteacher." Instead he nodded and asked the question he wanted to.

"Your mother all right?"

"No," said Denver. "No. No, not a bit all right."

"You think I should stop by? Would she welcome it?"

"I don't know," said Denver. "I think I've lost my mother, Paul D."

They were both silent for a moment and then he said, "Uh, that girl. You know. Beloved."

"Yes?"

"You think she sure 'nough your sister?"

Denver looked at her shoes. "At times. At times I think she was—more." She fiddled with her shirtwaist, rubbing a spot of something. Suddenly she leveled her eyes at him. "But who would know that better than you, Paul D? I mean, you sure 'nough knew her."

He licked his lips. "Well, if you want my opinion—"

"I don't," she said. "I have my own."

"You grown," he said.

"Yes, sir."

"Well. Well, good luck with the job."

"Thank you. And Paul D, you don't have to stay 'way, but be careful how you talk to my ma'am, hear?"

"Don't worry," he said and left her then, or rather she left editorial, written by a man, making light of, or challenging the widespread sexual abuse of women, or domestic violence against women. Can we imagine the firestorm that would have erupted over such a glaring and brutal example of sexism and misogyny? Instead, what we have is a firestorm over appropriation, which was not raised by the invited writers, with two camps arrayed against each other.

I am suggesting here that the debate about appropriation simultaneously erases and supplants the racist act that the publication of the editorial represents; further, it illustrates how systemic racism functions and how we can all be baited to participate in a debate that hides even as it reveals.

Yes, the issue of appropriation is a very real one—I might add here that living in the present, globalized, commodified world, there are very few of us who do not indulge or partake in practices of other cultures—from yoga to mindfulness meditation to Buddhism, to karate and other Asian martial arts. Is any of this appropriation? If not, why not? Further, Black culture—especially musical culture—has always been and continues to be appropriated by all cultures, bar none—Elvis Presley, Adele, Lily Singh, A Tribe Called Red, the Beatles, the Rolling Stones—the list is long. There appears to be no understanding that Black music bears a name, has an address and a particular and tragic history. Indeed, to use a digital example, Black culture is approached as if it is a creative commons to which everyone ought to have access. And it is a zero-sum game because the widespread consumption of Black culture has not resulted in any greater respect for the original creators. Indeed, in an extractive capitalist world, the opposite has been the result. Indigenous peoples have their own arguments about how their cultures have been appropriated as, I suspect, do all colonized cultures and peoples.

Appropriation is a complex issue, which often stems from a racist power structure which can do real harm to those who are racially, socially and politically marginalized. The debate over appropriation of voice, which this particular debate is all about, often lurches between those who are rightly concerned with the dangers of literary censorship on the one hand, and those who are concerned about very real damage that can be done by appropriative practices. There are those who argue that you cannot cage what is uncageable—the human imagination and inspira-

113

They get a name for idleness, and only earn
resentful spite from citizens.
The stupid ones, if you bring new ideas to them,
will view you as not clever but impractical.

And if you are perceived to be superior
to those who are supposed to be the subtle ones,
society will brand you as a troublemaker.
I myself have shared this fate:
because I'm clever, I am resented by some people,
and in some eyes I'm idle and in others opposite to that,
and for others I'm a nuisance.
Yet, in any case, I'm not so very clever.
But still, you say you are afraid of me—for what?
Becoming victim of some outrage?
No, don't be scared of me, Creon.
There is no call for me to do offense against the king.
What injury have you done me?
You gave your daughter to the man your heart proposed.
It is my husband; he's the one I hate:
your actions were, I think, quite sensible.
So now I don't begrudge your happy state—
go on, enjoy your wedding, and good luck to you all!
And let me live on in this country here—
since, even though I have been done injustice,
I'll hold my peace, subdued by those who have more power.

CREON

Your words are soothing to the ear;
but I still have a horror that inside your head
you're hatching plans for something bad.
I trust you all the less than I did previously.
A woman acting in hot blood
is easier to guard against—it is the same with men—
than one who's clever and stays secretive.
No—on your way immediately; don't give me speeches.

(85) MEDEA

PREFACE

Tragedy: A Curious Art Form

Why does tragedy exist? Because you are full of rage. Why are you full of rage? Because you are full of grief. Ask a headhunter why he cuts off human heads. He'll say that rage impels him and rage is born of grief. The act of severing and tossing away the victim's head enables him to throw away the anger of all his bereavements.[1] Perhaps you think this does not apply to you. You once in the city view with driving you to your mother's funeral, parked tab instead of right at the intersection and you had to scream at her so loud other drivers turned to look. When you tore off her head and threw it out the window they nodded, changed gears, drove away.

Grief and rage—you need to contain that, to put a frame around it, where it can play itself out without you or your kin having to die. There is a theory that watching unbearable stories about other people lost in grief and rage is good for you—may cleanse you of your darkness. Do you want to go down to the pit of yourself all alone? Not much. What if an actor could do it for you? They act for us. You sacrifice them to action. And this sacrifice is a mode of deepest intimacy of you with your own life. Within it you watch [yourself] act out the present or possible organization of your nature. You can be aware of your own awareness of this nature as you never are at the moment of experience. The actor, by reiterating you, sacrifices a moment of his own life in order to give you a story of yourself.

[1]. Renato Rosaldo, "Grief and the Headhunter's Rage," *Text, Play, and Story*, edited by E. M. Bruner (Washington, D.C.: American Ethnological Society, 1984), pp. 178–195.

You are mine
You are mine

I have your milk
I have your smile
I will take care of you

You are my face; I am you. Why did you leave me who am you?
I will never leave you again
Don't ever leave me again
You will never leave me again
You went in the water
I drank your blood
I brought your milk
You forgot to smile
I loved you
You hurt me
You came back to me
You left me

I waited for you
You are mine
You are mine
You are mine

no name?

VAMPIRIC CONSUMED consummation

consumption

perpetuation

"Mine" is a very bad word

geneal, and are politically

the fabulist, acknowing ~~this invention~~

~~Rumination concept action of the Cross Bronx Expressway,~~

on ~~shifting destination ready to be sent out for~~

production.

I'd like to spend my time at your institution

~~location of making, lurching between a threshold~~

writing and piecing together my next project, THOT. The ~~tive~~

THOT, is an ~~on-going~~ meditation, is an installation of ~~tragedy.~~

~~Whaing and outdoored~~ ~~already~~ that hope to ~~envision~~

the question, ~~elsewhere the~~ women go?

Several underlying questions ~~pushed~~ into the ~~economy of other things~~

including ~~but not far that is.~~

THOT, That. That. (that for short)

The word owns that, that has ~~met these~~

Where do the women go now?

Thank you for considering my application and I hope to join you

in the fall.

(The assumption is that can I ~~move people~~ ~~kill~~ ~~them off, and~~
~~and~~ ~~corruption~~ ~~is~~ ~~not based on~~ ~~they~~ ~~can't~~ ~~remedy~~, ~~I~~ ~~would find on~~
~~the real~~ ~~idea~~, ~~theorized~~ ~~to~~ ~~Plato~~, ~~with~~ ~~modern~~ ~~tyranny~~.)
~~take~~ ~~it~~ ~~...~~ ~~the page~~ ~~~~prove here~~

Alice is a desired undesirable woman

Who is doing the desiring

What constitutes the undesirable

Who decides

and what is a woman Lacan say Lacan is not The

Woman does not exist. I remember, ~~because~~ it's the only

phrase I know in French besides my own name which

isn't really French because it was given to me by my mother who

is from the Bronx.

~~I have set put the phrase on pretence of naming a child, let it sway~~
~~just a imprint, you in the pre-grief reckons we are, idea, so give something~~
~~place it exists it owes to the circulation, spill down, hang off, wander~~
~~exist. that's the whole point of Beloved. Bothe if between a man and a half place~~
~~he has Every last cousin Beloque. She has the children there – the boys, two girls. The~~
~~boys are good and they have names before they ever have any so. Names are all others~~
~~before the world without ever having to mention it us, we just gave them Names. they~~
~~~~names~~ ~~tries~~ ~~to~~ ~~make~~ ~~us~~ ~~believe~~ ~~we~~ ~~again,~~ ~~she~~ ~~wills~~ ~~get~~ ~~the~~ ~~pass~~ ~~for~~ ~~school~~ ~~teacher~~ ~~and~~ ~~the~~ ~~circulation~~

XVI.

Sethe sits with Beloved
            that shit
        her memory
                actions
                choices
            history, convinced
                    believing she had choices
                                actions
                        faults and it
                                        she drains
                                    feeds on
                                    kills
                                    suicide-by-cops, as though madness
                                                    blackness

gives an authority the right to kill a minority.

And we the community
            chorus are jealous
                    polite
                    policed
            heard
            flinched
            was writing
                staring at a story
                        paper
                    reflection.

Amanda calls:

You sound like Travis.

You look like Travis.

We need more space.

Facts.

Are you seeing somebody?

Faceless swipes on those apps, and a white girl with a boyfriend.

I meant like a professional.

Like a prostitute?

Like a doctor.

Oh—not yet, you?

Not yet.

Are you seeing somebody?

A man.

Really?

Why's that funny?

What's his name?

John.

Like a patron of prostitutes? Like a dead unclaimed
male body? Like a toilet? Like the fourth gospel?
Actually, did you know that in the military—I
remember because Leo's pops got one and ain't
been the same since but there's this thing called a
'Dear John Letter' which basically is shorthand for
like—iight so, say homie is deployed or like at work
or overseas. Whatever the situation, he's taking a
long break from his shorty. This shorty back home
writes him a letter because the term, I think, is before
phones and shit so they'd get these letters addressed
to them so I suppose they all had that name or like
because it's so common it becomes generic, and
applicable by default so the term is named after the
repeated action of addressing letters that were just
like yo' I've found love elsewhere, I won't be here
when and if you get back from killing.

You hear yourself? Hang up and text me so you can see what you're saying.

—Which when you really think about it, that's
probably the right decision because if homie

survives that, he's coming home crazy, isn't he? On average, they come home crazy? Prison, war—we come home crazy. They, I didn't mean to say we. I'm not saying that I think I'm at war. That'd be ridiculous. War and prison are not metaphors, right? I remember reading that somewhere. It's unethical to use war, prison, and slavery as metaphors even if you've heard shots, experienced confinement, and your body has been used for someone else's gain— it's still not okay to use war, prison, and slavery as metaphors, right?

There are institutions—

—Unfortunately, you don't have that power—which is interesting right because we're alive and present for gay marriage but, why would we do that? What happens when you're unmarried and of legal age? Do you know? I haven't seen, heard, read, flinched much about that—I try to stay away from psych papers because they don't seem to be written by humans. You think Danner might've been gay?

Your neighbor? Why are you always thinking about her? I have to clock-in. Text me.

Unfortunately, I'm not going to do that. I don't want to see what I'm saying just yet because if I see what I'm saying I'll agree with you, and I already know what's coming baby, I hear it, well kind of—every time I speak, I hear bullets, gun shots , *safety with*

a handsaw . How will I work if that's what I am?
Travis didn't work. My dad couldn't keep a real
job. Deborah Danner was killed in a subsidized
apartment.

Do you want to work?

No, but shouldn't I?

I don't think so.

Can you imagine?

Not really.

My mother's got "Perfect Attendance" awards framed
on her desk. There's pictures too but she's got perfect
attendance framed in gold.

Mine too and now me.

You should have taken more time off.

You think I could have? You get seven days for a brother, one month for a child. I took a second week but it came out my own pocket. You left.

This is time-sensitive, just like before with my dad,
and I didn't stop then; then, again with Danner. You
get nothing for a stranger. What was I supposed to

say—the girl I've been seeing on and off again since I was sixteen lost her little brother. Can I defer?

We're more than that and you could've tried, asked.

I probably could have but I don't talk to white people, especially not on Sundays. I just told you my voice sounds like bullets, gun shots to them too. I've never in seen a gun in real life, have you? How could I sound like something I've never seen?

We've heard them.

Government-issued or fireworks bought in Pennsylvania.

You're in love with a train stop. All you do is defend the hood.

'Til death do us part.

So why'd you run?

Run implies escape. I walked, I'm walking, sunday-strolling.

And does your Sunday-rule apply to white girls with boyfriends?

Send me my Dear John Letter and go. Is his name
really John? God, I hate that we just let anybody
name anything.

I'm just telling you that sounds dangerous, more dangerous than government-issued fireworks
bought in Pennsylvania. It sounds like suicide, stupid.

Fair Old Lady.

XVII.

Denver acts as hero

      heroine when she rallies the chorus

            community, asks them to stop being so jealous

                  polite

                  po-

liced. Her ability to see

      hear

      feel compassion

      sympathy

      relative morality suggests enhanced ability

            sense as though the same blood

                milk she drinks

that grants her immunity

      protection from that fate

            future

            history

          the baby

          Beloved also allows her to vanquish

                defeat

                stake

                release Beloved

                  history

                  future

                  fate, with voice

                    help

                    chants from a no longer

jealous
polite
policed chorus
     community.

    Come home.

            And be killed by the police or my mother?

Your mother is not going to kill you.

            Metaphorically.

Your mother is not going to kill you metaphorically.

            It's already happened like mad times, like mad
            times—that school, my pops' house. I don't know
            who dismissed, expelled, ousted me more, Clickety
            Clack with the keys or Barbara. Did you know
            I'm owed an expedition? I know it's still running.
            American cars require very cheap parts, very cheap
            labor.

Barbara isn't your mother.

            Right of course but she was my father's wife. And
            she has my expedition. And my mother sent me
            there, both places just for me to get kicked out over

and over and over again, and now I either sit too
still or I wander. What is a complacent fugitive? An
oxymoron.

You want the expedition, let's go get the expedition.

I don't want that shit. You know how cheap
American cars are? Besides, I think her boy drives
it. Nobody makes boys, forces boys to let shit go,
especially not expeditions.

Don't I know it.

Right, of course, I'm so sorry. I'm just—
*Girl, don't say sorry. Imagine if my mother had been half as hard on Travis as she had been on
me. Always so worried I'd become a hoe or something.*

I think she tried everything within her power.

I think yours did too.

There's still no excuse for sending me to that school.
Five days a week, ousted, dismissed, and told to
come back on Saturdays all because I'd rather take a
saw to my own neck than wear a skirt. Do you know
how ugly the UES is for a Black girl on a Saturday
morning?

You forget I was there too?

It was different for you.

You sound like a man.

Don't do that.

You acknowledged it once, in passing. Kind of. That girl from Astoria was in the third-floor bathroom crying about something that happened to her at one of those brother-sister school dances at Xavier. I think she got kicked out for a length-issue, I can't remember if it was her hair or her skirt. You said to her, those dances are for white people. Keep your Black ass out those dances, and then she cried-laughed and you said it's happened to all of us, and it really was all of us—every Black girl in the school fit into that third-floor bathroom, so yes it was more than just you, not much more but still.

A Black girl from Astoria?

That's not the point. I don't know Queens, maybe it was something else but I remember your joke and then your whisper. Do you remember?

Don't start asking me about my memory. I'll never get anything done if you do.

You brought it up. For someone that doesn't want to work, you sure like to get things done.

Complacent fugitive owed an expedition.

XVIII.

Gender separates

    divides

        distinguishes Denver from her brothers quite obviously

                      , and Morrison could have stopped there if drink-
ing the milk

      blood of the baby weren't enough reason

                    explanation for staying

                        not leaving 124

                        her enhanced ability

                              power

                              guilt

                              sense of responsibility,

but Morrison continues

      writes more

      gives Denver a prophet's

          protagonist's

          hero's birth

                 origin story. Could you imagine having enough power to give
a Black girl, within a tragedy

        realistic novel, a hero's birth?

It's crazy that you ask me things, talk to me so much, remember with me now.

              We're both off on Sundays.

What was it you said your grandmother said about you, jokes and grass? I hope we don't lose
touch.

Like lack feeling?

Like stop talking.

Why would we ever stop talking?

Well yours may have a boyfriend but mine wants to be a boyfriend.

So is monopolizing your Sundays more or less
suicidal than white girls with boyfriends?

Fair but he's harmless, just dumb.

That's not nice.

I like him because he's dumb. I mean it as a compliment. Dumb is the wrong word. He's—
Simple. Sane. Is he nice to you?

Complicated. He called me a Thot the last time I was out there to visit you.

Visiting me makes you a thot ?

I packed thongs.

He was there to watch you pack? That's intimate.
You couldn't find a Michael? "St. Michael, defend us

in battle. Be our protection against the wickedness and snares of the devil." St. Michael gets shit done, b. John, the baptist, John the Baptist, "grant unto Thy people the grace of spiritual joy, and direct the minds of all Thy faithful into the way of everlasting salvation." John, the baptist, Amanda—come on, not John the Baptist. Baptist church is eight hours long, like a work-day, in a skirt, and when I wouldn't wear one, Barbara would whisper to my father as though anyone could whisper around me let alone people whose natural, normal tone was shouting, praising but still she'd whisper "get her out of here" "take her home" which was actually fine. I really do hate Brooklyn and you know at the end of that, they all like convene and eat say the right words and shit which we know I can't do but, I can hear you, I can hear you say I don't belong. This is also why I think I'm owed that expedition. Who spent more time in that car than me? I know that's not how law works but, shouldn't it?

Have you been talking like this in public? Slipping in and out of time? Your mother know you been talking like this?

My mother , like yours, is at work. Am I bothering you? I thought today was Sunday.

Jack and Jill went up the hill to fetch a pail of water—

—Jack fell down and broke his crown and Jill came tumbling after.

I know that, Amanda. I'm not crazy. I k . Are you saying I should be grateful for having a father who tried and a mother not stupid enough to go tumbling after? I admit, it's a pretty decent combination and still.

Everything else is just the world and when has the world been kind to us?

Facts.

XIX.

Denver

Amy Denver finds Sethe in a forest

        space

        time between Sweet Home and 124. She's a good story

            folktale

            memory from

neither

between time

    space

    settings. Her sole purpose is to usher Sethe to safety

        a canoe

        rub feet and deliver a baby

            Denver, give her her name and

disappear. Has Morrison reversed yet another trope

        stereotype and created a Magical White

            —Well, she is

in no way a negro by any standard

    accepted

    authoritative

    white definition of the word.

Because I have been understood (by Amanda), I make the mistake of believing I'm understandable and start speaking

    biting

      talking back

          to authorities

              voices

              white girls with boyfriends, even on Sundays.

Authorities:

    Do you know why I've pulled you over

                        "'Cause I'm young and I'm black and my hat's real low?
                        Do I look like a mind reader, sir? I don't know.
                        Am I under arrest or should I guess some more?"

    Well you were doing 65 in a 64

                        No let me finish that line for you, because I really feel
                        you lack the necessary rhythm to truly carry it out:

                        "License and registration and step out of the car"
                        "Are you carrying a weapon on you, I know a lot of
                        you are?"

    Is this some kind of joke to you?

                        Trope?

    Joke.

                        Either way—yes.

Voices:

>abandoned
>mistreated
>misused
>beat
>a witness.

>>That's not how you listen.

I feel you.

>>That's not how you show listening.

Word?

>Danner
>Schizophrenia

>Bullet holes and institutions
>>churches
>>signs

>>buildings. I'm Black and—

>>>You're trained.

Sell
Tell to whom?
>Who is listening to me?

I am. It's Polka dots for a friend of mine back home.

White girls with boyfriends:

> from between her legs
>> arms
>> lips.

> *You see yourself in everything clear, even my wetness.*

> Damn, that's crazy.

I'm not crazy. You're reckless, narcissistic, endangering yourself and others.

> And the crowd goes wild. I didn't call you crazy.

There's nobody here but me.
> 'Damn, that's crazy' just means I'm not re-
ally listening
   willing to engage with that thought
            that I don't agree
            I'm not trying to argue with you. I sound like bullets
                        gun shots but they're
fucking placebos
   pellets
   government-issued fireworks.

Narcissistic is what I said. You don't hear how you sound to others?

Is that something I should be able to do?

Of course—

I'll leave, we can text. Sometimes I can't hear but I can always read.

It's the sounds

It's Narcissism.

Do you know the story of Echo and Narcissus?

I know he died staring at himself.

Do you know what comes before that?

It doesn't matter to the present conversation.

Right, of course. Did I make you up?

You really believe you're God when you stare at a screen, invincible and omnipotent.

Well speaking of gods, there's so much before the actual point of Narcissus staring at himself to death.

Back to the myths. You speak in quotes. You don't even see that I'm here trying to have a real-life, present conversation with you.

The Margaret Garner Incident happened in 1856.
Deborah Danner was killed in 2016. I'll stop
speaking in quotes when quotes
echoes stop happening.

What incident?

Deborah Danner?

No, I've heard you talk about her before.

Then you've heard me talk about Margaret Garner
before. I talk about it all at the same time. The
Modern Medea.

That's a greek myth.

What isn't? You just called me narcissistic.

*All I'm saying is if I or anyone like me used a name that was traditionally Black for something
else—*

—What's a name that's traditionally Black?

I don't know, your name or like—

—My name is appropriated as well I suppose if we're
tracing and tracking and thinking in terms of who
owns what and who was owned by what but I don't
necessarily disagree with you—about my name

being traditionally Black. I think it is traditionally Black to do France better than France. Have you been to New Orleans?

Americans don't know anything outside of America.

When you says 'Americans,' you mean me?

Yes, of course.

I'm not arguing. I was just curious. I don't think I've ever been grouped with 'Americans' before, at least not by a white person.

Calm down. You don't have to get mad at me.

Why do you think I'm mad?

XX.

Like Beloved
Denver too rises from the river—

go home
walk down the hill
Castle Hill Avenue, talk:

We were talking about Narcissus because she was calling me narcissistic and so I wanted to like respond and explain the math of that. Like the identity property essentially but I was making jokes, pulling up grass, taking too long to get to like the variables and factors and well, you know what I mean—

    No.

                How's the baptist?

The Thot-calling never stopped, so.

                You mean like you felt called to be a Thot and
                therefore—

No like he never stopped calling me that. I mean that sounds like what she was attempting to call you too but—

Facts b. She certainly wasn't really describing the narcissus myth, or like maybe she was and it is. Have you ever called me narcissistic?

Probably but I mean—

—Nah I get that but would you mind if I continued the conversation with you or is that like fucked up?

It's fucked up, but what do you mean you just want to talk about the Narcissus myth?

Yes.

Shoot.

Well how do we know he was staring at his reflection when he could have just been staring at the river? Are rivers beautiful to Gods and Nymphs? Probably not because from their perspective—it's common and regular and always there and sure maybe he's beautiful and special to them and himself but just because something is clear and common to Gods and Nymphs doesn't mean it's clear and common for us. Water is mad beautiful, B and nobody owns it. At least not then—can you imagine a time before water was owned?

Staring at your own reflection or actually just taking a moment to reflect.

Thank you, yes, that's what I'm trying to say.

Most intellects do not believe in god but they fear us just the same. You like that song right?

Yeah, I do.

Sources

Carson, Ann. "Preface." *Grief Lessons: Four Plays*, 7. New York: New York Review Books, 2006.

Euripides. "Medea." *Euripides I*, 85. trans. Oliver Taplin. Chicago & London: The University of Chicago Press, 2013.

Morrison, Toni. *Beloved*, 242, 256, 314. New York: Vintage Books, 1987.

Nourbese Philip, Marlene. "Race-Baiting and the Writers' Union of Canada." *Bla_k*, 113. Ontario: Book*hug, 2017.

Chanté L. Reid is a writer from the Bronx, New York. She holds writing degrees from both Brooklyn College and Brown University, and has been an adjunct instructor up and down New England.

Sarabande Books is a nonprofit literary press located in Louisville, Kentucky. Founded in 1994 to champion poetry, short fiction, and essay, we are committed to creating lasting editions that honor exceptional writing. For more information, please visit sarabandebooks.org.